What Are the Consequences of Climate Change?

Andrea C. Nakaya

San Diego, CA

© 2017 ReferencePoint Press, Inc.
Printed in the United States

For more information, contact:
ReferencePoint Press, Inc.
PO Box 27779
San Diego, CA 92198
www. ReferencePointPress.com

LIBRARY OF CONGRESS CATALOGING-IN-PUBLICATION DATA

Names: Nakaya, Andrea C., 1976-
Title: What are the consequences of climate change? / by Andrea C. Nakaya.
Description: San Diego, CA : ReferencePoint Press, Inc., 2017. | Series:
    Issues in society | Audience: Grade 9 to 12. | Includes bibliographical
    references and index. | Description based on print version record and CIP
    data provided by publisher; resource not viewed.
Identifiers: LCCN 2016020653 (print) | LCCN 2016012225 (ebook) | ISBN
    9781682820797 (eBook) | ISBN 9781682820780 (hardback)
Subjects: LCSH: Climatic changes--Juvenile literature. | Climate change
    mitigation--Juvenile literature.
Classification: LCC QC903.15 (print) | LCC QC903.15 .N35 2017 (ebook) | DDC
    577.2/2--dc23
LC record available at https://lccn.loc.gov/2016020653

CONTENTS

A Changing World

Kiribati is a small republic that comprises thirty-three low-lying islands located in the Pacific Ocean. In recent years nations around the globe have become increasingly concerned about the consequences of climate change. However, for the people of Kiribati, the issue is more than a future concern. Climate change is already having a dramatic impact on the everyday lives of the more than one hundred thousand people who live in this island nation. The Intergovernmental Panel on Climate Change (IPCC), a multinational organization that monitors environmental data, stated in a 2014 report that the global mean sea level rose by about 7.5 inches (19 cm) between 1901 and 2010 due to climate change and predicted that levels will continue to rise another 1 to 4 feet (30 to 122 cm) by 2100. The rise in sea levels is due to global warming, a heating up of the earth that melts polar ice caps and ice sheets in nations like Greenland and raises water temperatures, both of which cause the oceans to expand. Kiribati is only a few feet above sea level, so as the sea rises, parts of the islands are disappearing underwater, and freshwater supplies and farmland are being contaminated by salt water.

Many people fear that as a result, Kiribati will ultimately disappear. Kiribati president Anote Tong says, "The science is telling us we really have a problem ahead of us. The projected scenarios of sea-level rise are not good for us." He claims that some smaller Kiribati communities will soon be forced to relocate, and he warns, "Maybe in 50 years, we are talking about the entire nation."[1] As a result of such predictions, the country has even purchased a large piece of land in nearby Fiji as a possible place to grow food and relocate some of its population. The plight of Kiribati, where people fear that their entire country may disappear, is an extreme case. However, it illustrates how a changing climate can have a massive impact on humanity.

What Is Climate Change?

To understand climate change, one must understand the role of climate as both a local and global phenomenon. *Climate* means the general, long-term weather patterns that characterize an area, and whether stable or changing, it affects every living thing on earth. A region's climate includes things such as average rainfall and temperature, typical humidity, and average wind speed. A stable climate is beneficial to most plants, animals, and people because it provides consistent and reliable living conditions on which they can depend. For example, people in India and Southeast Asia rely on yearly summer monsoon rains to water the crops that provide most of their food. Joshua trees, which live in the

Global temperature increases are causing the earth's oceans to warm and bodies of ice and snow to shrink. Here, massive icebergs from Jakobshavn Glacier in Greenland are slowly melting on a summer evening.

Mojave Desert of the United States, are another example of how living things depend on a predictable climate. These plants thrive in hot desert conditions, but they also depend on a period of cold weather every winter in order to reproduce. Unexpected changes in the climate can threaten survival by leaving plants and animals in conditions to which they are unaccustomed and poorly suited to survive. For example, if average temperatures rise in the Mojave Desert, the Joshua tree may no longer receive the cold winter weather it needs to reproduce. Or if weather patterns in India and Southeast Asia change, monsoons could become more intense, and too much rain can wash away crops and bring dangerous flooding.

> "The evidence for rapid climate change is compelling."[2]
>
> —NASA.

While climate is never completely static, in general the earth's overall climate has remained relatively stable for hundreds of years; and plants, animals, and humans have all adapted to living in fairly predictable conditions. However, now there is mounting evidence that this period of stability may be over because the climate is beginning to change. The consensus of the IPCC's hundreds of experts is that there is no doubt that climate change is occurring and is dramatically affecting the earth. The IPCC says that global temperatures are rising, oceans are warming and rising, bodies of ice and snow are shrinking, and weather patterns are changing. Other researchers, scientists, and organizations all over the world agree. For instance, the National Aeronautics and Space Administration (NASA) says, "The evidence for rapid climate change is compelling,"[2] and the European Environment Agency insists, "Climate change is happening now."[3]

The Future of Humanity Is Connected to Climate Change

Because life is so closely tied to climate, a changing climate is a threat to humankind's way of life. While most people take it for granted, climate affects every part of their lives, including what they eat, where they live, the type of energy they use, their health, and what they do for work and for recreation. The US Environmental Protection Agency (EPA) stresses, "Our lives are connected to the climate." It warns that because of this strong connection, climate change is likely to force a change in people's everyday lives: "A warming climate will bring changes that can affect our water supplies, agriculture, power and transportation systems, the natural environment, and even our own health and safety."[4] Dramatic changes in everyday life have already happened in Kiribati. However, in most other parts of the world, the effects of climate change have been far less pronounced. Whether Kiribati is a sign of things to come or a rare example is uncertain. Overall, most people agree that climate change will affect humankind, but there is still widespread disagreement about exactly what those effects will be and whether humankind can do anything to change this future.

CHAPTER 1

What Are the Facts?

Northern Africa's Sahara Desert is one of the largest deserts in the world. Much of it receives less than 1 inch (2.5 cm) of rain every year, and its inhospitable landscape is sparsely populated. Yet based on analysis of sediment samples, researchers believe that as recently as six thousand years ago, this area was actually lush and green, with numerous lakes. Cave paintings from the Sahara are believed to show watering holes and an abundance of animal life where there is now only sand and rock. As this example makes clear, climate change is a fact of life on earth. Geologic evidence shows that the earth's climate has not and does not remain the same; it has changed many times in the past. For example, certain parts of the world have transformed from wet to dry or hot to cold. NASA says, "The Earth's climate has changed throughout history. Just in the last 650,000 years there have been seven cycles of glacial advance and retreat."[5] According to NASA, the last glacial period—or ice age—ended about seven thousand years ago, and since then the earth's climate has been relatively stable. However, NASA and most scientists believe that despite this period of stability, the climate is unlikely to remain as it is. Instead, it is generally agreed that just as it has changed in the past, the earth's climate will change again at some point in the future.

A Complex System

The earth's climate is determined by a complex interactive system that comprises many elements, including the sun, atmosphere, oceans, landmasses, plants, and living creatures. The sun is one of the most important parts of the climate system because it is the source of most of the earth's energy. NASA describes just how much energy the sun produces. "Averaged over an entire year, approximately 342 watts of solar energy fall upon every square meter of Earth," the organization says. "This is a tremendous amount of energy."[6] By comparison, NASA explains that a large electric power plant creates about 1 billion watts of power. It would take 44 million of these power plants to create the same amount of energy that comes from the sun.

The atmosphere is another important part of the climate system because it helps determine what happens to all that energy. Not all of it stays on the earth. The atmosphere traps some but also allows some of it to escape back into space. The gases in the atmosphere that trap energy are often called greenhouse gases because they act like a greenhouse to keep in heat and keep the earth warm. Greenhouse gases are very important for life on earth; without some gases to trap heat, the earth would be too cold to live on. However, if the concentration of greenhouse gas was too high, the earth could be too warm to live on. In a chapter of *Climate Change: What It Means for Us, Our Children, and Our Grandchildren*, John T. Abatzoglou and other climate experts explain how different concentrations of greenhouse gases have resulted in drastically different temperatures on other planets. They state, "The thick, carbon dioxide–rich (97 percent CO_2) Venusian atmosphere is highly effective at keeping thermal radiation from escaping to space, resulting in an average surface temperature of 470°C (878°F)." They explain, "In contrast, Mars has a very thin atmosphere with a minimal greenhouse effect. As a result, most of the heat radiated from the surface of Mars escapes to space, and the average surface temperature on Mars is about -60°C (-76°F)."[7]

> "The Earth's climate has changed throughout history. Just in the last 650,000 years there have been seven cycles of glacial advance and retreat."[5]
>
> —NASA.

Water vapor, carbon dioxide, methane, and nitrous oxide are the major greenhouse gases in earth's atmosphere. Water vapor is the most common and is not influenced significantly by human activity. It does not stay in the atmosphere very long, because it is constantly falling down to the earth as precipitation. The amounts of the other greenhouse gases are determined in part by human activity and can stay in the atmosphere much longer—up to hundreds of years. Carbon dioxide is the next most common after water vapor, and it comes largely from the burning of fossil fuels.

Climate change is dramatically affecting the earth, leading to global temperatures rising and changing weather patterns such as severe storms and droughts. Here, nomads walk by a dried-up river during a drought in the Sahara Desert.

Methane comes from livestock farming and agriculture, as well as the production and transport of natural gas. Nitrous oxide comes from agriculture and from burning fossil fuels. The more that humans burn fossil fuels and expand agriculture, the more these gases build up in the atmosphere.

Other Influences

The planet's oceans are also important to the climate. Since oceans cover 71 percent of the earth's surface, it is the oceans—particularly at the equator—that receive the bulk of the sun's energy. They redistribute that energy around the earth. The National Oceanic and Atmospheric Administration (NOAA) explains:

Ocean currents act much like a conveyer belt, transporting warm water and precipitation from the equator toward the poles and cold water from the poles back to the tropics. Thus, currents regulate global climate. . . . Without currents, regional temperatures would be more extreme—super hot at the equator and frigid toward the poles—and much less of Earth's land would be habitable.[8]

While water is dark in color and absorbs heat, some parts of the oceans are frozen into ice, such as in the Arctic. These stretches of ice also influence climate because they reflect heat back into the atmosphere, helping cool the planet.

Another important part of the climate system is the earth's forests, which influence atmospheric levels of carbon dioxide and thus the overall level of greenhouse gases. Trees absorb carbon dioxide from the atmosphere through photosynthesis, so large areas of forest reduce the amount of carbon dioxide in the atmosphere. In contrast, deforestation increases atmospheric carbon dioxide because there are fewer trees to absorb this gas. Because they take so much carbon dioxide from the atmosphere, trees contain large amounts of stored carbon. This means that deforestation further increases atmospheric carbon dioxide, because when trees are cut down and burned they release all their stored carbon into the atmosphere. Current rates of deforestation are high. According to the Food and Agriculture Organization of the United Nations, between 2000 and 2010, 12.8 million acres (5.2 million ha) of forest were lost per year around the world.

Forests also impact the climate by influencing rainfall patterns. The earth has an ongoing water cycle by which water evaporates into the atmosphere and then falls down again as rain. Forests play a major role in that cycle by helping generate rainfall, and areas without forests are much more likely to be dry. Researchers have found that changing rainfall in one area can actually impact weather patterns around the world. For example, according to a 2013 study by Greenpeace, computer models indicate that deforestation in the Amazon could reduce spring and summer rain in Texas by 25 percent but increase rainfall in the Arabian Peninsula up to 45 percent.

In addition to all the individual components of the climate system, such as forests and oceans, the earth's climate can be dramatically affected by processes called feedback loops. Feedback loops occur when a change in one part of the climate system interacts with other components, which can result in a much larger change. For example, ice reflects a lot of heat back into space. However, when the earth's ice sheets melt during a period of warming, there is less area to reflect heat, so more planetary warming occurs. This means that even more ice melts, and the cycle continues. Another example of a feedback loop is happening to the Arctic tundra. In some parts of the Arctic, the ground stays frozen all year and is called permafrost. However, as the climate warms, much of this permafrost is beginning to melt. Huge amounts of greenhouse gases are trapped in the permafrost, and when it melts, these gases are released into the atmosphere. This results in more heat being trapped on earth and increased temperatures, which causes more permafrost to melt.

Greenhouse Gases and Temperatures

While every part of the climate system is important, many scientists pay particular attention to greenhouse gases because they believe these gases are a key factor in determining what happens to the climate. There is evidence that over the past few hundred years, the concentration of greenhouse gases in the earth's atmosphere has increased substantially. Since the late 1950s, scientists have been measuring the atmospheric carbon dioxide concentration from the top of the Mauna Loa volcano in Hawaii. This record shows that carbon dioxide levels have been steadily rising since measurement began, from less than 320 parts per million (ppm) to more than 400 ppm.

> "Every year we report a new record in greenhouse gas concentrations."[9]
>
> —Michel Jarraud is secretary-general of the World Meteorological Organization.

Other greenhouse gases have been continually increasing, too. World Meteorological Organization secretary-general Michel Jarraud says, "Every year we report a new record in greenhouse gas concentrations."[9] The major causes of greenhouse gases are the burning of fossil fuels and industrial processes. According to the IPCC, between 1970 and 2010, 78 percent of the total increase

Greenhouse gases such as carbon dioxide and nitrous oxide, which come from the burning of fossil fuels, play a role in climate change. Here, cars clog the roads during rush-hour traffic in Beijing, China, increasing the carbon dioxide in the atmosphere.

in the world's carbon dioxide emissions came from industrial processes and fossil fuel combustion.

Some people use the analogy of a bathtub with a partially closed drain to explain how carbon dioxide and other greenhouse gases build up in the atmosphere. The water in the bathtub represents the level of greenhouse gases in the atmosphere. The drain represents the things that take greenhouse gases out of the atmosphere, such as oceans and plants. The faucet represents the gases pouring in from things like the burning of fossil fuels. If more gases pour in than can drain out, then the level in the bathtub steadily rises. This is what seems to be happening to the earth.

There is evidence that higher concentrations of greenhouse gases are correlated with higher temperatures. Scientists have found this evidence by drilling samples from deep in the Arctic ice in order to construct a historical record of the earth's atmosphere over thousands of years. These ice core samples have air bubbles, which contain the different particles and gases that were in the atmosphere when the bubbles were formed. Analysis of these samples shows that at times when carbon dioxide levels were higher, so was the earth's temperature, and when they were lower, the earth was cooler. Record keeping from more recent times also reveals a similar pattern: As greenhouse gases have steadily increased in the past hundred years, world temperatures have also increased.

Climate Is Changing

Whether or not greenhouse gas concentrations are to blame, the fact is that researchers all over the world have observed major changes in the past hundred years to the earth's climate and environment and are extremely concerned about the implications of these changes. Due to widespread concern, in 1988 the United Nations Environment Programme and the World Meteorological Organization created a scientific body to study exactly how the climate is changing and how it might affect the environment and humankind. This scientific body—the IPCC—is now the world's foremost authority on climate change. The work of the IPCC is conducted by hundreds of experts from all over the world, who review and assess all the existing evidence on climate change and produce reports. The first report was issued in 1990. Reports were also issued in 1995, 2001, 2007, and the most recent in 2014.

In its most recent report, the IPCC concludes that climate change is significant. It says, "Warming of the climate system is unequivocal, and since the 1950s, many of the observed changes are unprecedented over decades to millennia." The IPCC reports that both land and ocean temperatures are gradually increasing. It says, "Each of the last three decades has been successively warmer at the Earth's surface than any preceding decade since 1850. The period from 1983 to 2012 was likely the warmest 30-year period of the last 1400 years in the Northern Hemisphere."[10] Overall, the report says that between 1880 and 2012, the climate has warmed by a little less than 2°F (1°C). This might not sound like much, but as the National Geographic Society explains, even a small tempera-

> "Warming of the climate system is unequivocal, and since the 1950s, many of the observed changes are unprecedented over decades to millennia."[10]
>
> —The IPCC.

Geoengineering

Some people believe it is possible to actively manipulate the world's climate and thus reduce warming through a process called geoengineering. There are two main ways that geoengineering scientists have focused on cooling the earth: the first is by taking carbon dioxide out of the air, and the second is by reducing how much of the sun's energy actually reaches the earth. Various methods have been proposed to accomplish these goals. One is to fertilize the ocean with iron, which would stimulate the growth of plankton so that they will absorb more carbon dioxide from the air. Another is to inject sulfur particles into the atmosphere to reflect sunlight back into space. However, while such ideas have been widely discussed, scientists recognize that the consequences could be unpredictable. As Mike Hulme, a professor of climate and culture at King's College London, says, "To embark on this course of action would indeed be to conduct a giant experiment, to take a leap in the dark." As a result of such uncertainty, geoengineering has not received widespread public support.

Mike Hulme, *Can Science Fix Climate Change? A Case Against Climate Engineering*. Malden, MA: Polity, 2014, p. 112.

ture change can be significant. For example, it says that during the sixteenth and seventeenth centuries, average global temperatures were about 2°F to 3°F (1°C to 1.7°C) cooler than today, but this was enough to cause what is referred to as the Little Ice Age. The publication explains, "A change of one or two degrees might not seem like a lot, but it was enough to cause some pretty massive effects. For instance, glaciers grew larger and sometimes engulfed whole mountain villages. Winters were longer than usual, limiting the growing seasons of crops. In northern Europe, people deserted farms and villages to avoid starvation."[11] The IPCC believes that the current period of warming is also likely to greatly affect both the earth's physical environment and its living things.

Shrinking Ice and Rising Oceans

Many substantial changes have already been observed. One is that as the earth's land and ocean temperatures have increased, its bodies of ice have shrunk significantly. The earth contains some extremely large areas of ice; the Greenland and Antarctic ice sheets are the two largest ice sheets in the world. According to the National Snow & Ice Data Center, the Antarctic ice sheet is approximately the same area as the contiguous United States and Mexico combined. The Arctic also contains a large area of ice. Parts of these bodies of ice remain frozen year-round, whereas other areas freeze in the winter and melt in the summer. However, data shows that every year, more ice is melting and less is refreezing. For example, according to the IPCC, the extent of Arctic sea ice has decreased every season since 1979. In 2013 researchers from the NOAA predicted that Arctic summers will become almost ice free by the middle of the twenty-first century.

Scientists can construct a record of the earth's atmosphere over thousands of years by analyzing ice core samples, which contain gases that were in the atmosphere when the ice formed. Here, a scientist drills for ice core samples on a glacier in Iceland.

Volcanic Eruptions and Climate

Volcanic eruptions can significantly impact the climate because they release large amounts of sulfur dioxide into the atmosphere. The gas condenses into particles that reflect sunlight back into space, and it thus has a cooling effect on the climate. Most volcanic eruptions are too small to have a noticeable effect on the climate; however, according to the US Geological Survey (USGS), there have been some very large eruptions in the past that actually lowered the earth's surface temperature up to half a degree Fahrenheit (.28°C) for up to three years. The USGS describes the effects of the 1991 eruption of Mount Pinatubo in the Philippines:

> [The eruption] injected a 20-million ton (metric scale) sulfur dioxide cloud into the stratosphere at an altitude of more than 20 miles. The Pinatubo cloud was the largest sulfur dioxide cloud ever observed in the stratosphere since the beginning of such observations by satellites in 1978. . . . It was a standout in its climate impact and cooled the Earth's surface for three years following the eruption, by as much as 1.3 degrees F at the height of the impact.

US Geological Survey, "Volcanoes Can Affect the Earth's Climate," February 26, 2016. http://volcanoes.usgs.gov.

As bodies of ice around the globe shrink, the level of the ocean is rising. This is because ice is turning into water and adding volume to the ocean, and also because as ocean water warms, it expands. While measurements differ by location, according to the IPCC, between 1901 and 2010 sea level rose by an average of about 7.5 inches (19 cm) worldwide. There is also evidence that the rate at which it is rising is accelerating. According to *National Geographic*, over the past twenty years, the annual rate of rise was about twice the rate of the eighty years before that.

An Uncertain Future

The potential effects of climate change are believed to be so significant that many nations are taking action to address this threat. Most recently, representatives from 195 nations, including the

United States, met in Paris for a climate change conference in 2015. They agreed that the world should try to prevent the global climate from increasing more than 3.6°F (2°C) above preindustrial temperatures and that in order to do so, there must be major reductions in worldwide greenhouse gas emissions. Most experts believe that if the temperature does increase more than 3.6°F (2°C), the world will be locked into an irreversible future of extremely harmful climate-related effects such as severe storms and droughts and the mass extinction of plants and animals. In Paris national representatives submitted climate action plans that detail how they plan to do their part in reducing greenhouse gases, and they agreed to give regular reports on their progress toward those goals. While many critics charge that the agreement is not enough, there are also many supporters who believe that it is a good start toward international recognition of the issue and cooperation toward addressing it. After the agreement was made, UN secretary-general Ban Ki-moon said, "The Paris agreement on climate change is a monumental success for the planet and its people."[12] As of this writing the agreement had not yet been ratified.

"The Paris agreement on climate change is a monumental success for the planet and its people."[12]

—Ban Ki-moon is the secretary-general of the United Nations.

Despite global concern and actions such as the Paris agreement, most data indicate that climate change has not slowed, and experts generally agree that it is part of humanity's future. There is much less agreement about what is causing climate change, how severe the change will be, and how it will affect life on earth.

2 Is Climate Change a Serious Problem?

Most climate scientists agree that throughout history there have been numerous dramatic changes to the earth's climate. There is evidence of multiple ice ages, in which ice and snow covered most of the world, including much of North America. There is also evidence of periods of time when the climate has been warmer than it is now, even warm enough to completely melt the polar ice caps. Modern society has not experienced any of these drastic changes though, because they occurred thousands of years ago. Instead, society has evolved during a period of time when the climate has remained somewhere in the middle—not too hot and not too cold. Under these moderate conditions, humans have flourished and the world's population has become larger than ever before. However, there is evidence that this period of stability is ending and the climate is changing. There is a large amount of uncertainty about what the extent of this change will be and what it means for humankind. Some people fear that climate change is a serious threat, while others contend that it is normal for the earth's climate to undergo periodic change. Nobody knows for sure what the future holds.

Disagreement on Climate Trends

Some people believe the future will be bleak. They insist that humans are creating such a large quantity of greenhouse gases that they are causing drastic and irreversible change to the climate. This argument is based on the belief that greenhouse gases are the major cause of climate change and that human activity, such as the burning of fossil fuels, is causing the level of greenhouse gases in the atmosphere to increase year after year. These gases are believed to be causing dramatic changes to the climate now, and it is thought that they are likely to cause continuing change in the future. NASA warns that the level of greenhouse gases already in the atmosphere is so high that a major change in earth's climate has already been set in motion. The agency explains:

> Even if we stopped emitting greenhouse gases today, global warming would continue to happen for at least several more decades if not centuries. That's because it takes a while for the planet (for example, the oceans) to respond, and because carbon dioxide—the predominant heat-trapping gas—lingers in the atmosphere for hundreds of years. There is a time lag between what we do and when we feel it.[13]

Critics contend that the climate is too complex to be influenced by human activity and that current changes in the climate are simply part of a natural cycle that humans have no control over. Geologist E. Kirsten Peters insists that it is normal for both short-term and long-term climate changes to occur. She explains that this has happened again and again over thousands of years. She says, "Earth's global climate reverses, staggers, and stumbles, again and again." In her opinion, "The Earth looks like she may be overdue for another, fully natural, climate revolution."[14] She believes that humans have nothing to do with this change and have no power to alter it. However, critics like Peters are in the minority, and most scientists believe that human activity has influenced the climate.

> "The Earth looks like she may be overdue for another, fully natural, climate revolution."[14]
>
> —E. Kirsten Peters is a geologist.

Whether or not climate change is human caused, many climate experts worry that this change is a serious threat because it seems to be happening so quickly. Climate expert G. Thomas Farmer argues that while the climate has gone through major changes in the past, these changes have happened slowly, over hundreds and thousands of years, which gave people time to adjust. In contrast, he states that modern society may face sudden, drastic changes. He warns, "In the next 100 years into the future

Above, California residents paddle down a flooded street after heavy rains caused the San Diego River to overflow its banks. Many scientists fear that climate change will cause the sea level to rise, putting coastal areas at risk of flooding or even disappearing into the ocean.

our children and grandchildren and all future generations could be the first ever to experience a climate of as much as 6°C or more above pre-industrial temperature."[15] To highlight the potential magnitude of this change, he points out that at present the climate has only changed by about 2°F (1°C). As a result of this small change, he says, "familiar weather patterns are being disrupted, polar ice sheets are melting, sea ice around the North Pole is disappearing, storms are becoming more intense, tropical diseases are spreading into higher latitudes and altitudes, and seasons of the year are changing . . . and all because of 1°C." He wonders, "What will happen with 2, 3, 4, 5, 6, or 10°C?"[16]

Rising Oceans

As the climate warms, many scientists fear that sea level will rise substantially, threatening low-lying island nations and coastal cities. Researchers have found it difficult to predict exactly how high the sea will rise. However, the IPCC estimates that sea level will rise at a higher rate than in the past fifty years, and it could be anywhere from about 1 foot (30 cm) to close to 4 feet (122 cm) higher

Climate Change Is the Result of Solar Variation

Some people believe that the earth is so sensitive to the sun's energy output that variations in that energy are actually the major cause of earth's changing climate. In a 2015 research paper, Willie Soon of the Harvard-Smithsonian Center for Astrophysics and independent research scientists Ronan Connolly and Michael Connolly argued this point.

For thousands of years, researchers have considered the possibility that changes in solar activity can lead to climate change on Earth. [For example, Greek philosopher] Theophrastus (371–287 BC) suggested there might be a connection between sunspots and rain and wind. . . . However, without systematic and quantitative measurements and records with which to check these possibilities, any such theories remained mostly speculative. [According to our data-based analysis] it seems that most of the temperature trends since at least 1881 can be explained in terms of solar variability, with atmospheric greenhouse gas concentrations providing at most a minor contribution. This contradicts the claim by the latest Intergovernmental Panel on Climate Change (IPCC) reports that most of the temperature trends since the 1950s are due to changes in atmospheric greenhouse gas concentrations.

Willie Soon, Ronan Connolly, and Michael Connolly, "Re-Evaluating the Role of Solar Variability on Northern Hemisphere Temperature Trends Since the 19th Century," *Earth-Science Reviews*, August 11, 2015. www.friendsofscience.org.

by 2100. This means that many areas will be at risk of flooding, and some coastal towns and cities may even be completely swallowed by the ocean. For instance, in the 2014 National Climate Assessment, researchers reported that almost 5 million people in the United States live within 4 feet (122 cm) of the local high-tide level, so they are likely to experience flooding as the sea rises. In a study published in the journal *Nature Climate Change* in 2016, researchers warned that the potential effects are even greater and that up to 13 million Americans could experience flooding by the end of the century. National Climate Assessment researchers also caution that the problem is likely to keep worsening for a long time. They predict, "Sea level rise will not stop in 2100 because the oceans take a very long time to respond to warmer conditions at the Earth's surface. Ocean waters will therefore continue to warm and sea level will continue to rise for many centuries at rates equal to or higher than that of the current century."[17] The USGS warns that if the world's major ice sheets melted completely, the sea could rise as much as 260 feet (79 m).

The Pacific Ocean has many low-lying island nations that are already experiencing destruction from rising seas and increasingly

Climate Change Is Not the Result of Solar Variation

While most scientists recognize that the sun plays a critical role in the earth's climate, many, like the writers of *Skeptical Science*, insist that it is not the cause of recent climate changes. *Skeptical Science* is a blog that challenges the arguments made by those who deny that climate change is real.

> As supplier of almost all the energy in Earth's climate, the sun has a strong influence on climate. A comparison of sun and climate over the past 1150 years found temperatures closely match solar activity. However, after 1975, temperatures rose while solar activity showed little to no long-term trend. . . . In fact, a number of independent measurements of solar activity indicate the sun has shown a slight cooling trend since 1960, over the same period that global temperatures have been warming. Over the last 35 years of global warming, sun and climate have been moving in opposite directions. An analysis of solar trends concluded that the sun has actually contributed a slight cooling influence in recent decades.

Skeptical Science (blog), "Sun & Climate: Moving in Opposite Directions," December 24, 2015. www.skepticalscience.com.

VIEWPOINT

powerful storms. For example, most of the land in the Marshall Islands is less than 6 feet (1.8 m) above sea level, and it is common for residents there to see salt water and raw sewage flooding their streets and homes during a storm. Journalist John D. Sutter visited these islands and stresses that they are so close to sea level that for their approximately seventy thousand residents, there is literally no escape from rising seas. He says, "In the nine days I spent in Majuro, the crescent-shaped capital of the Marshall Islands, I learned there is nowhere on these islands to escape the floods. People, I was told, seek shelter on the second stories of buildings, or by climbing up the trunks of coconut trees. The only 'hill' to speak of in Majuro is a bridge that's built over an inlet."[18] US president Barack Obama warns that some islands could disappear completely, forcing their residents to move elsewhere. He says, "We might deal with tens of millions of climate refugees in the Asia Pacific region."[19]

Yet some researchers contend that although a rising ocean might mean destruction in some places, it may compensate by creating new land in other places. Geomorphologist Paul Kench has been researching reef islands in the Pacific and Indian Oceans and argues that rising seas do not necessarily mean that the islands there will vanish. Together with colleagues in Australia and Fiji, he found that many islands actually move and change shape as coral grows and sediments move around. In fact, he found that as the sea has risen in recent years, some islands have actually grown larger. *National Geographic* journalist Kennedy Warne explains the findings of Kench and his colleagues: "Their analysis, which now extends to more than 600 coral reef islands in the Pacific and Indian Oceans, indicates that about 80 percent of the islands have remained stable or increased in size. . . . Only 20 percent have shown the net reduction that's widely assumed to be a typical island's fate when sea level rises."[20] Critics of climate change doomsayers argue that such data show that the earth has the

> "We might deal with tens of millions of climate refugees in the Asia Pacific region."[19]
>
> —Barack Obama is the forty-fourth president of the United States.

ability to adapt to climate change in surprising ways and that rising seas may not actually cause the widespread harm that most people assume.

Weather Extremes

In addition to sea level changes, some people believe that climate change will drastically change weather patterns around the world. Meteorologists have observed that as the temperature increases, the amount of moisture in the atmosphere increases. This additional moisture impacts the weather. For instance, when rain and snow occur, they are likely to be heavier. In addition, while there is more precipitation in some areas, the extra moisture in the atmosphere changes air-circulation patterns, intensifying droughts in other regions. Finally, more moisture in the atmosphere—along with warmer oceans—can make hurricanes more intense. Many researchers expect that all of these weather changes will occur if the climate warms in the future. Overall, researchers predict more intense weather around the world, including stronger storms,

Some researchers argue that rising seas may cause reef islands in the Pacific and Indian Oceans to change shape and possibly even grow larger as corals grow and sediments move around. Pictured is an island in the South Pacific Ocean.

more heat waves and other temperature extremes, and dramatic changes in rainfall, resulting in both droughts and flooding.

There is evidence that extremes are already occurring. The 2014 National Climate Assessment gives numerous examples of recent weather extremes. For example, according to the report, the number of heat waves in the United States has been increasing. In 2011 and 2012 the number of intense heat waves was almost triple the long-term average, with Texas and the Midwest setting records for highest monthly average temperatures. Overall, the report states, "Prolonged (multi-month) extreme heat has been unprecedented since the start of reliable instrumental records in 1895."[21] It also states that heavy precipitation events have increased; for instance, since 1991 there has been an increase of more than 30 percent above the 1901–1960 precipitation average in the Northeast, the Midwest, and the upper Great Plains.

A *National Geographic* article describes how in 2010, Nashville, Tennessee, experienced record flooding due to extreme pre-

Some scientists believe that climate change may increase the frequency and intensity of hurricanes. Pictured is a satellite photo of Hurricane Katrina, which made landfall in August 2005 and was one of the deadliest and most intense hurricanes in US history.

cipitation. According to journalist Peter Miller, when the storm was over, parts of Nashville had received more than 13 inches (33 cm) of rain, which was twice as much as the previous record. Singer and songwriter Brad Paisley says that millions of dollars of musical equipment was ruined in the flooding. "Every amp, every guitar I'm used to, was destroyed," he says, "I felt powerless in a way I've never felt before with weather." Paisley says that the flood made him think twice about assuming that the weather will always be the same as it has been in the past. He says, "Since that flood, I've never once taken normalcy for granted."[22]

While many researchers agree that climate change will make extreme weather more common, there is less agreement about how it will affect hurricane activity in the future. Massachusetts Institute of Technology hurricane specialist Kerry Emanuel argues that hurricanes will become more frequent and more intense as a result of climate change. He used six different climate models from the IPCC and combined them with a hurricane model to generate predictions about future hurricane activity. He presented his findings in a 2013 paper, arguing that there will be a 10 percent to 40 percent increase in hurricane frequency by 2100. In addition, he found that storms may be up to 45 percent more powerful. In contrast, some scientists believe that although hurricanes might get stronger, they are likely to be less numerous. In a 2015 report, the Geophysical Fluid Dynamics Laboratory, a laboratory of the NOAA, stated that climate change may increase the number of very intense hurricanes in some areas. However, it also predicts that the overall number of hurricanes worldwide is likely to either decrease or remain about the same.

Critics Say Predictions Are Exaggerated

In response to predictions of increasingly dangerous storms, weather extremes, and rapidly rising seas, some critics contend that the threat of climate change has been greatly overstated. The Nongovernmental International Panel on Climate Change (NIPCC) is one such critic. This organization was founded in 2003 by a group of scientists and scholars who believe that the IPCC's predictions are not based on good science, because the organization is heavily influenced by political interests. In reports issued in 2013 and 2014, the NIPCC says that its team of approximately fifty scientists has evaluated the evidence and come to the conclusion that IPCC predictions about future warming are exaggerated. Instead, the NIPCC says, "Any warming that may occur is likely to be modest and cause no net harm to the global environment or to human well-being."[23]

Academic Bjørn Lomborg is also critical of climate change predictions. He argues that discussions about climate change often tend to focus on the negatives and ignore other data. He says, "Many climate-change alarmists seem to claim that all climate change is worse than expected. This ignores that much of the data are actually encouraging." For example, he says that there is research showing that the rate at which the ocean is rising has decreased, as has the number of droughts. He says, "In short, climate change is not worse than we thought. Some indicators are worse, but some are better. That doesn't mean global warming is not a reality or not a problem. It definitely is. But the narrative that the world's climate is changing from bad to worse is unhelpful alarmism."[24]

Another common critique of climate change predictions is that the computer models used to create many of these predictions are inaccurate. While scientists can collect hard physical data to understand the past and current climates, it is impossible to know exactly what the future climate will be like. As a result, many predictions about the climate come from complex computer models. For these models, scientists create programs that imitate the way various elements of climate such as ocean currents and rainfall work. Then they put in estimates of future changes such as increased levels of greenhouse gases and see what the resulting climate changes might be. However, critics of these models insist that the climate is so complex that it is impossible to accurately model it. The NIPCC explains, "The science literature is replete with admissions by leading climate modellers that [some things that influence climate] are not sufficiently well understood, that data are insufficient or too unreliable, and that computer power is insufficient to resolve important climate processes."[25] As a result, the NIPCC says that it is impossible to create a model that accurately simulates many elements of the climate system, such as clouds, wind, precipitation, ocean currents, and sea ice. Without accurate simulations of these important elements, scientists cannot predict the future climate.

Overall, there continues to be widespread debate over whether climate change is a serious problem. This disagreement is not limited to scientific experts; polls show that there are also differing views among the American public. For instance, a 2015 Gallup Poll of American adults showed a complete lack of agreement concerning news reports on climate change. Forty-two percent of respondents said that the seriousness of climate change is exaggerated in the news, 35 percent believe it is underestimated, and 21 percent said that news reports are generally correct. Climate change continues to be an extremely controversial and divisive issue, and the only way to settle the debate is to wait and see what the future holds.

"Any warming that may occur is likely to be modest and cause no net harm to the global environment or to human well-being."[23]

—The NIPCC is an organization that analyzes research about climate change.

Will Climate Change Threaten the Survival of Plants and Animals?

Polar bears live exclusively in the Arctic region of the world. They eat mainly seals, capturing them when the seals come up to breathe through holes in the sea ice. Polar bears hunt on the ice all winter. In the summer when the ice has melted, they return to land, where they survive on fat stored from their winter meals. Unfortunately, the Arctic climate is changing, with the sea ice becoming thinner and melting sooner every year. As a result, polar bears are having more trouble finding enough food in the winter, and many are starving to death. The International Union for Conservation of Nature estimates that there is likely to be at least a 30 percent reduction in the population of polar bears within three generations. As the Arctic becomes progressively warmer every year, many scientists worry that polar bears are ultimately headed toward extinction. Polar bears are not the only creatures threatened by climate change. All over the world, plants and animals are experiencing new challenges as their environments change. With the climate expected to continue changing in the future, scientists wonder whether these plants and animals will be able to adapt or whether their survival is threatened.

Adaptation

Some experts insist that climate change is not a serious threat to the survival of plants and animals because many will be able to adapt to changes. Australian geneticist Ary Hoffmann points out that adaptation is a normal part of life for living things. "Organisms are not static," he says. Unfortunately, says Hoffmann, most predictions about the future ignore that fact. "Most of the models that ecologists are putting out are assuming that there's no adaptive capacity. And that's silly,"[26] he insists. Instead, point out critics like Hoffmann, change is a natural part of life, and many species evolve over time. The IPCC reports that this is happening as the climate changes, with many species in both land and water evolving in multiple ways, including where they live, their migration patterns, seasonal activities such as breeding, and the various species they interact with. In a 2011 report in the journal *Science*, researchers describe the results of their analysis of how plants and animals are shifting in range, or the geographic areas that they live in. They found that as the climate warms, species are migrating to cooler locations. These species are moving to higher elevations by approximately 36 feet (11 m) per decade and to higher latitudes at about 10 miles (16 km) per decade. Biologist Chris D. Thomas insists that there is a definite relationship between warming and migration. He says, "The more warming there's been in an area, the more you would expect a species to move, and the more they have moved."[27]

"Most of the models that ecologists are putting out are assuming that there's no adaptive capacity. And that's silly."[26]

—Ary Hoffmann is an Australian geneticist.

The quino checkerspot butterfly is an example of how living creatures can prove to be surprisingly adaptable. In 2014 researchers reported that the butterfly had shown rapid and unexpected adaptation to climate change, defying previous predictions that it would soon become extinct. Originally, the butterfly was abundant in Mexico and Southern California. However, rising temperatures reduced the number of plants that its caterpillars feed on, and some scientists believed that the quino checkerspot would become extinct unless humans took action to relocate it. Before such relocation plans could be carried out, however, the butterfly surprised everyone by relocating itself. It moved to higher altitudes and chose a different species of plant to lay its eggs on. "Every butterfly biologist who knew anything about the quino in the mid-1990s thought it would be extinct by now, including me,"[28] says Camille Parmesan of the Marine Institute at Plymouth University. Instead, Parmesan and others now see the butterfly as proof that scientists may be underestimating the ability of plants and animals to adapt to climate change.

In some cases movement and adaption can even lead to an overall increase in the number of plant and animal species.

Due to changes in the climate, Arctic sea ice is becoming thinner and melting sooner each year. As a result, polar bears are having more trouble finding food in the winter, and many starve to death.

Thomas describes how this can happen. He says that the warmer temperatures and increased rainfall that climate change is causing in many areas do mean that certain species that are adapted to the cold will no longer be able to survive there. However, he explains that while a small number will be lost, the altered climate supports a larger number of new species. He argues that overall, a warmer area is able to support a larger number of different species than a colder area. "On average, less than one native species dies out for each introduced species that arrives," he says. "Britain, for instance, has gained 1,875 established non-native species without yet losing anything to the invaders."[29] In addition, Thomas explains that diversity also increases through hybridization. This happens when formerly separated species are brought into contact and breed together to create new hybrid species. Overall, Thomas believes that ecological diversity could actually increase in the future as the climate changes.

Problems with Rapid Change

While it is true that living creatures have proved their ability to adapt in surprising ways, critics fear that because climate change is occurring so rapidly, it will make adaptation too difficult for many. Conservationist and author William deBuys says, "One response is to say that this kind of thing has happened over and over again through the ages of evolutionary change," and he agrees that it has. However, he argues that the current period of climate change is unique. He explains, "The difference now is the speed of the change, which threatens to outstrip the adaptive capacity of many creatures, as well as the systems in which they are enmeshed."[30] DeBuys and others fear that climate change is occurring so quickly that many creatures will not be able to adapt quickly enough to survive.

Rapid climate change is already causing problems for living creatures all over the world. One problem is that weather changes are resulting in mismatches between two species that have traditionally depended on one another. For instance, ecologist Lee Hannah says that a rise in temperatures in the Rocky Mountains has caused marmots to come out of hibernation earlier. However, it has not caused the snow to melt or plants to flower earlier. As a result, he says, "[There is] a 23-day mismatch between emergence of marmots and their food plants."[31] This means that marmots are starving. Another problem is that migration is causing different species to cross paths for the first time, and this can have negative effects. For example, Arctic foxes have always lived on the Arctic tundra, but as the weather becomes warmer, they are facing competition from red foxes, which are migrating into their territory. Red foxes are larger and generally more powerful, so when the two species compete for food in the same place, the red fox usually gets the food and the Arctic fox goes hungry.

> "The difference now is the speed of the change, which threatens to outstrip the adaptive capacity of many creatures, as well as the systems in which they are enmeshed."[30]
>
> —William deBuys is a conservationist and author.

Species Loss

As a result of challenges such as these, some plants and animals are threatened with extinction. Many scientists believe that as the climate changes, worldwide extinction rates will be high. The IPCC warns, "A large fraction of species faces increased extinction risk due to climate change during and beyond the 21st century."[32] The Center for Biological Diversity also believes that extinction rates will be high. It states, "We're currently experiencing the worst spate of species die-offs since the loss of the dinosaurs 65 million years ago."[33] Sea turtles are one species threatened by the changing climate. Whether sea turtle eggs hatch into females or males usually depends on the temperature of the sand they are laid in, with warm beaches resulting in more females. This means that a warming climate is likely to result in fewer male turtles, and this threatens the species' future survival. The Sea Turtle Conservancy reports that at Playa Grande, on the Pacific coast of Costa Rica, turtle nests are 70 percent to 90 percent female. At Junquillal Beach, also on Costa Rica's Pacific coast, the organization says that it is often too hot for the eggs to even hatch.

"We're currently experiencing the worst spate of species die-offs since the loss of the dinosaurs 65 million years ago."[33]

—The Center for Biological Diversity is a nonprofit conservation organization.

While living creatures have proved to be remarkably adaptable to change, they have also shown that they can be extremely vulnerable. Hannah discusses the extinction of the golden toad in Costa Rica, which he says was the first documented extinction due to climate change. His example shows just how quickly a creature can go extinct. The golden toad was abundant in the rain forest for many years, and researchers were able to observe it easily when toads congregated in huge numbers to mate each year. However, as the climate changed, the rain forest became drier, and this change caused the golden toad to suddenly become extinct. Hannah says, "In 1987, the mating aggregation failed to materialize and the golden toad was never seen again. Just that quickly, from one year to the next, the entire species vanished."[34]

If large numbers of plants and animals do become extinct, scientists warn that biodiversity will be reduced and that this will be harmful to all living things, including humans. Biodiversity is the existence of many different plant and animal species within a particular ecosystem. All of these species play an important role in keeping the system functioning and healthy. In the National Climate Assessment, researchers explain how important biodiversity is to humankind. The assessment says, "Biodiversity and ecosystems produce a rich array of benefits that people depend on, including fisheries, drinking water, fertile soils for growing crops, climate regulation, inspiration, and aesthetic and cultural values. These benefits are called 'ecosystem services.'. . . Ecosystem services contribute to jobs, economic growth, health, and human well-being."[35] An example of an important ecosystem service is the way that people use plants to create medicines. According to the World Wide Fund for Nature, approximately fifty

The golden toad of Costa Rica was once abundant in the rain forest, but when climate change made the rain forest drier, the toads quickly became extinct.

The Earth Is Facing a Mass Extinction Event

In a 2014 article in *Science*, researchers affiliated with a number of different universities around the world argued that human activity may be leading to what they called a sixth mass extinction. They explained that humans are causing climate change, habitat destruction, and other harms that are steadily eliminating the world's species.

In the past 500 years, humans have triggered a wave of extinction, threat, and local population declines that may be comparable in both rate and magnitude with the five previous mass extinctions of Earth's history. Similar to other mass extinction events, the effects of this "sixth extinction wave" extend across taxonomic groups, but they are also selective, with some taxonomic groups and regions being particularly affected. . . . So profound is this problem that we have applied the term "defaunation" to describe it. This recent pulse of animal loss, hereafter referred to as the Anthropocene defaunation, is not only a conspicuous consequence of human impacts on the planet but also a primary driver of global environmental change in its own right.

Rodolfo Dirzo et al., "Defaunation in the Anthropocene," *Science*, July 25, 2014. http://science .sciencemag.org.

thousand to seventy thousand different plant species are harvested for medicines worldwide. Reduced biodiversity means that important ecosystem services such as this may no longer exist.

Trouble in the Ocean

The threat of species loss and reduced biodiversity is not a concern just on the land. Climate change is also having a dramatic effect on the health of the oceans and the creatures that live in them. Researchers have discovered that the oceans are absorbing large amounts of carbon dioxide from the atmosphere, which is making them more acidic. According to the Smithsonian National Museum of Natural History, ocean water has become 30 percent more acidic in the past two hundred years. This increased acidity is causing harm to many ocean creatures. For example, coral and sea creatures with shells need calcium carbonate to make those hard structures. Higher levels of carbon dioxide in the ocean water make it difficult for these creatures to extract the calcium carbonate they need, and they are unable to make shells, or they make shells that are weaker. Even creatures that do not make shells may be harmed by increased acidity. For example, the Smithsonian explains that even small changes in the level of acid in the water can have a big impact on important chemical reactions that occur in the bodies of fish. It describes research on

The Earth Is Not Facing a Mass Extinction Event

Some critics argue that predictions of mass extinctions are nothing new and that these predictions always turn out to be exaggerated. Award-winning science writer Ronald Bailey believes that current predictions will likewise turn out to be overstated.

> This is not the first time biologists have sounded the alarm over allegedly accelerated extinctions. In 1970, S. Dillon Ripley, secretary of the Smithsonian Institution, predicted that in 25 years, somewhere between 75 and 80 percent of all the species of living animals would be extinct. . . . In 1975, the biologists Paul and Anne Ehrlich wrote that "since more than nine-tenths of the original tropical rainforests will be removed in most areas within the next 30 years or so, it is expected that half of the organisms in these areas will vanish with it.". . . The late 20th century's predictions of imminent mass extinction happily proved wrong. The positive trends [to protect animals] provide good grounds to believe that the new ones will also turn out to be exaggerated.

Ronald Bailey, "Predictions of a Man-Made Sixth Mass Extinction May Be Exaggerated," *Reason*, August 1, 2014. www.reason.com.

VIEWPOINT

clown fish, reporting, "Even slightly more acidic water may also affect fishes' minds. While clownfish can normally hear and avoid noisy predators, in more acidic water, they do not flee threatening noise. Clownfish also stray farther from home and have trouble 'smelling' their way back."[36] The Smithsonian believes these behavioral changes may be the result of acid changing the way that the fish's brain processes information.

In addition to carbon dioxide, researchers have found that the oceans are also absorbing large amounts of heat and thus becoming progressively warmer. This is having a disastrous impact on the health of coral reefs, they say, and when coral reefs become sick, the overall health of the oceans is threatened. Coral reefs are some of the most diverse ecosystems in the world, and they are vitally important to oceans because thousands of ocean creatures rely on them for survival. According to the NOAA, while coral reefs cover less than 1 percent of the ocean, they support approximately 25 percent of marine life. As a result of rising ocean temperatures, coral reefs around the world are becoming sick because of something called bleaching. Normal healthy coral has a symbiotic relationship with microscopic algae; the coral protects the algae, and the algae provide the coral with important nutrients. However, when the water gets too warm, the coral expels the algae. This is called bleaching because losing the algae makes coral lose its color. In addition to leaving coral colorless, the process weakens or kills it. This is what is happening to coral around the world. For instance, in 2015 NOAA scientists announced that record ocean temperatures were causing a massive coral bleaching event that would kill about one-third of the world's coral by the end of the year.

> "It is clear that major extinctions have resulted from past climate change.
> . . . Yet some major climate changes have not resulted in extinctions."[37]
>
> —Lee Hannah is an ecologist.

Extinction Predictions May Be Exaggerated

Despite evidence that many plants and animals are being harmed by climate change, some scientists believe that extinction predic-

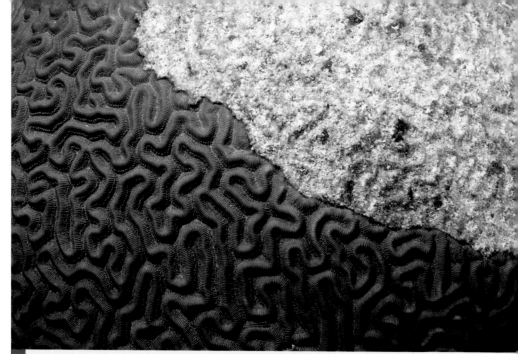

Rising ocean temperatures lead coral reefs to expel the algae that normally provide nutrients, leaving the corals weakened and colorless—a process known as bleaching. The white area of this brain coral has been bleached and is covered by sediment.

tions have been greatly exaggerated. They argue that there is no hard evidence to back up these dire predictions. Instead, they insist that predictions about extinction are simply guesses, because there has never been a period of climate change precisely like the one earth is now experiencing. Hannah maintains that an examination of those climate changes that have occurred in the past provides conflicting evidence. He says, "It is clear that major extinctions have resulted from past climate change. . . . Yet some major climate changes have not resulted in extinctions."[37] According to Hannah and others, because the current changes in climate are unique, there is no way to know for sure what will happen to the world's plants and animals.

Other researchers argue that extinction predictions are incorrect because they are based on incorrect estimates of the total number of different species that exist on earth. Nobody knows for sure how many different species of plants and animals there actually are in the world. In 2013 New Zealand researchers published a report arguing that the real number is significantly lower than previously thought. They explain that this has significant implications for estimates about future extinctions. This is because when researchers believe a particular habitat contains more species than it really does, then the rate of extinction also appears to be higher than it really is. The New Zealand researchers believe that as a result of overestimating the total number of species, predictions about extinction may have been significantly overestimated. One of the researchers, Mark Costello, says, "Our findings are potentially good news for the conservation of global biodiversity."[38] Costello and his fellow researchers believe that extinction is still a threat; however, they think that if there is a smaller number of total species than previously thought, it will be easier for scientists to identify them and try to save them from extinction.

Overall, there is strong evidence that the world's plants and animals are being affected by climate change. Some are facing extinction, and many others are being forced to alter where and how they live. However, predictions about the future vary. Some people forecast devastating declines and extinctions, while others insist that life will adapt and evolve.

Will Climate Change Impair Human Health and Well-Being?

The tiny village of Newtok is located on the west coast of Alaska, on the shores of the Ninglick River. It was established in 1959—less than sixty years ago. However, it is rapidly disappearing, and its approximately 350 residents are in the process of trying to relocate to a new piece of land 9 miles (14.5 km) away. Newtok is vanishing because Alaska's climate is changing. Every year temperatures there are rising and storm surges are becoming increasingly powerful, and as a result, the river is rapidly eroding the village. Experts believe that the whole village will soon be underwater.

Suzanne Goldenberg, an environmental correspondent for the *Guardian* newspaper, spent time in Newtok. She says, "Every year during the storm season, that river can take away 20, 30, [even] up to 300 feet a year. . . . It just rips it off the land, away from the village in these terrifying storms."[39] According to Goldenberg, "The people of Newtok . . . are living a slow-motion disaster that will end, very possibly within the next five years, with the entire village being washed away."[40] However, relocating an entire village is very expensive, and while Newtok residents voted in 1996 that it was necessary, most of them are unable to afford the cost. So they remain where they are, watching as their village slowly falls apart. Their plight is an example of how climate change can significantly harm human health and well-being. Alaska is feeling the effects of climate change more intensely than many other parts of the world; however, most experts believe that no matter where they live, all of the world's people will ultimately be impacted in some way by climate change.

Disagreement over the Extent of the Threat

There is less agreement over precisely what the impacts will be and whether climate change poses a serious threat to humanity. The IPCC admits that thus far the effects of climate change on human health are relatively minor, with both negative impacts—such as increased deaths from heat waves—and positive effects, such as fewer cold-related deaths. However, the IPCC and many other experts predict that this will change as the climate becomes warmer. Many see a future where changes in the climate will be extremely harmful to human health and well-being. The IPCC warns, "Globally over the 21st century, the magnitude and severity of negative impacts are projected to increasingly outweigh positive impacts."[41] The World Health Organization (WHO) estimates that climate change will cause about 250,000 extra deaths every year between 2030 and 2050, and that by 2030 climate change–related health costs will reach $2 billion to $4 billion a year. WHO director Maria Neira says, "The impact of climate change on human health is, indeed, alarming. Around the world, variations in climate are affecting, in profoundly adverse ways, the air we breathe, the food we eat and the water we drink. We are losing our capacity to sustain human life in good health."[42]

> "The impact of climate change on human health is, indeed, alarming."[42]
>
> —Maria Neira is the director of WHO.

Critics contend that the threat to human health has been greatly exaggerated. Not only do they believe that the problems caused by climate change will be much less severe than predicted, but they also argue that humans are resourceful enough to find solutions that will drastically reduce the impact of the things that do threaten them. Indur M. Goklany, former US delegate to the IPCC, explains that the prediction of negative effects

> ignores the fact that people and societies are not potted plants; that they will actually take steps to reduce, if not nullify, real or perceived threats to their life, limb and well-being. Thus, if the seas rise around them, heatwaves become more prevalent, or malaria, diarrhoeal disease and hunger spread, they will undertake adaptation measures to protect themselves and reduce, if not eliminate, the adverse consequences.[43]

Goklany and others argue that people have already proved their ability to adapt to climate change–related threats. For example, as the climate warms, the mosquitoes that spread malaria are expanding into new areas of the world, but Goklany says that global mortality rates for malaria have actually been significantly reduced in the past sixty years. He insists that nations that have the money for technology and research will find effective and affordable solutions to many of the other threats that will come with climate change.

Vector-Borne Diseases

One of the specific areas of concern for climate change and health is how it will affect the spread of disease around the world. Vector-borne diseases are a major concern, since they are already a big problem in many countries and have proved to be sensitive to climate. Vector-borne diseases are spread by vectors such as fleas, ticks, and mosquitoes; and they include such life-threatening conditions as West Nile virus and malaria. As the climate becomes warmer, the vectors that spread these diseases are able to expand into areas where they were previously unable to survive. Warm weather can also increase vectors' numbers by allowing them to mature more quickly and to have a longer breeding season. Researchers have found that many vector-borne diseases are already moving into new parts of the world as the climate warms. For example, the National Institute of Environmental Health Sciences reports that two types of mosquitoes that carry malaria can now be found at the US border with Mexico.

The Zika virus is an example of the devastation that can be caused by a vector-borne disease. This virus is spread by mosquitoes, and while it often causes only mild illness, some researchers believe that pregnant women who are infected with Zika are more likely to have babies with microcephaly. Microcephaly is a condition in which infants have smaller heads and incomplete brain development. As the Zika virus has become increasingly common in Brazil, so have cases of microcephaly in infants. From 2014 to 2015 cases of microcephaly there increased from 147 to almost 4,000. Because of this huge increase, WHO has declared

Some researchers believe that a Zika virus infection during pregnancy can make women more likely to have babies with microcephaly, a condition in which infants have smaller heads and incomplete brain development, such as the infant pictured above.

Zika to be a public health emergency, and many South American countries have warned women to delay pregnancy because of the threat of the virus. For instance, in 2016 El Salvador advised women to delay getting pregnant until 2018. There have not yet been any reported cases of Zika transmission resulting from mosquitoes found in the United States. Thus far all US cases have been travel-related but, experts believe this will change.

Other Health Threats

Experts believe that climate change is also likely to affect the spread of food-borne and waterborne diseases. Like vector-borne diseases, food-borne and waterborne diseases are a serious health threat in many countries, particularly, less developed ones. For example, cholera kills hundreds of people in many African nations every year. WHO reports that worldwide, cholera deaths total 28,000 to 142,000 people each year. Food-borne and waterborne illnesses like cholera spread when food or water become contaminated with disease-causing microorganisms such as bacteria and viruses. Researchers believe that climate change may increase the spread of food-borne and waterborne diseases because when temperatures are higher, the microorganisms that cause these diseases grow more quickly. These types of illnesses are also more likely to occur when there is heavy precipitation, which is another anticipated consequence of climate change. This is because heavy rainfall can wash pathogens into water supplies, where they make people sick.

It is also believed that climate change may deteriorate air quality in many places, which could increase rates of allergies, asthma, and other respiratory problems. There are numerous reasons that air quality is expected to worsen. First, the higher temperatures anticipated in the future will likely increase levels of smog and other air pollutants. Climate change is also predicted to cause increased precipitation in many areas, which will increase mold, another respiratory irritant. While heavy precipitation is expected in some places, other areas are expected to see increased drought, which increases the chance of wildfires, another cause of air pollution. Finally, warmer temperatures are expected to increase pollen levels, which are expected to increase allergies. WHO estimates that about 2 million people already die every year from air pollution, and it predicts that climate change will cause this number to rise.

Threats from Extreme Weather

In addition to affecting the spread of disease, climate change could also threaten human health through extreme weather. Many climate change researchers believe that climate change will bring more flooding, droughts, heat waves, and storms. All of these threaten human health. Extreme heat is one of the most harmful types of extremes. According to the National Weather Service, heat is one of the primary weather-related killers in the United

States and causes hundreds of deaths every year. Heat waves can kill by causing heat exhaustion and heat stroke, in addition to exacerbating serious health conditions such as kidney disease and cardiovascular disease. Some extreme heat waves in various parts of the world have killed thousands of people at a time. For example, in 2010 a record-breaking heat wave in Russia killed more than fifty thousand people.

Extreme precipitation can also cause serious problems. The National Climate Assessment states that floods are one of the deadliest weather-related hazards in the United States. In addition to causing drownings and widespread destruction of property, the flooding that often results from heavy precipitation can spread disease. Bangladesh, a very densely populated low-lying country located next to India, often experiences flooding. Richard A. Matthew, who has authored numerous publications about climate change, explains that flooding threatens the health of thousands of people there. He gives the example of the monsoon season in 2004, stating, "The coastal region of Bangladesh was paralyzed by severe flooding. By mid-July, 60 percent of the country was under a blanket of water soiled with a rank mixture of industrial, agricultural, and household waste. Some 20 million people were directly affected, many of them facing food and fresh water shortages, skin infections, disease, and displacement."[44] If climate change does increase heavy precipitation events in places like Bangladesh, problems such as these are likely to intensify in the future.

Benefits of Weather Changes

Critics point out that there is still widespread disagreement over whether climate change will lead to an increase in future weather extremes. For example, in 2015 the American Meteorological Society published its fourth annual report investigating the link between climate change and extreme weather. Researchers examined thirty-two extreme weather events in 2014. While they found that some of these events were more likely to occur or likely to be more intense because of climate change, for many weather extremes they found no connection. "The studies this year are pretty evenly

Here, rickshaws and pedestrians make their way through a submerged street after heavy monsoon rains caused flooding in Bangladesh. Extreme precipitation and flooding such as this can lead to serious problems such as drownings and the spread of disease.

split, about 50-50, for those that did and did not find a role for climate change in the event's likelihood or intensity,"[45] says NOAA climate scientist Stephanie Herring. Skeptics argue that such a lack of evidence means there is no good reason to believe there will be future weather extremes that will threaten human health.

Some researchers argue that humankind will actually be lucky if the climate does warm, because they believe the alternative may be worse for humanity. Geologist E. Kirsten Peters explains that a look at earth's past as seen in the geologic record reveals that earth's climate has naturally swung back and forth between periods of warmth and ice ages. Based on historical patterns, she believes that the current period of warmth has been relatively long, and a change is inevitable. "If the Earth continues to behave as she has for the past two million years, we must expect a return to bitter cold at some point,"[46] she says. Peters and others insist that such cold would harm far more people than warm temperatures would. They argue that warming would be a welcome historical change because of the problems associated with past ice ages.

Climate Change Is Already Reducing Food Security

Some people believe that climate change is reducing food security around the world. In a 2014 report, researchers from the IPCC, an international organization that monitors and assesses climate change data, commented on this worrisome trend.

> The effects of climate change on crop and terrestrial food production are evident in several regions of the world (high confidence). Negative impacts of climate trends have been more common than positive ones. . . . Since AR4 [the IPCC's 2007 report], there have been several periods of rapid food and cereal price increases following climate extremes in key producing regions, indicating a sensitivity of current markets to climate extremes, among other factors. . . . Several of these climate extremes were made more likely as the result of anthropogenic emissions (medium confidence). . . . Climate trends are affecting the abundance and distribution of harvested aquatic species, both freshwater and marine, and aquaculture production systems in different parts of the world. . . . These are expected to continue with negative impacts on nutrition and food security for especially vulnerable people, particularly in some tropical developing countries.

J.R. Porter et al., "Food Security and Food Production Systems," in *Climate Change 2014: Impacts, Adaptation, and Vulnerability. Part A: Global and Sectoral Aspects. Contribution of Working Group II to the Fifth Assessment Report of the Intergovernmental Panel on Climate Change*, ed. C.B. Field et al., 2014. www.ipcc.ch.

An example of the devastation caused by crushing cold is found in a period that scientists refer to as the Little Ice Age. The Little Ice Age is believed to have occurred between the early fourteenth and late nineteenth centuries, and it caused extremely cold conditions around the world. For example, the New York City harbor froze for the first time ever in 1870, and people could walk between Staten Island and Manhattan. The extreme cold caused crops to fail and led to widespread food shortages. History professor Geoffrey Parker talks about the seventeenth century, one of the coldest parts of the Little Ice Age. He says that in addition to famine, the cold precipitated all kinds of problems. He explains:

Few areas of the world survived the 17th century unscathed by extreme weather. . . . North America and West Africa both experienced famines and savage wars. In India, drought followed by floods killed over a million people in Gujarat between 1627 and 1630. In Japan, a mass rebellion broke out on the island of Kyushu following several poor harvests. Five years later, famine, followed by an unusually severe winter, killed perhaps 500,000 Japanese.[47]

Climate Change Is Not Reducing Food Security

Julian Morris, vice president of research at the Reason Foundation, argues that climate change has not reduced food security. Instead, he insists that food security has actually improved in most of the world and will continue to do so.

Pessimists claim that climate change is already reducing food availability. But the trend is in the opposite direction. Over the course of the past half-century, improvements in agricultural technology have dramatically increased food production. For example, cereal yields have nearly tripled, from 0.6 tons per acre in 1961 to 1.7 tons per acre in 2013. As a result, per capita food availability is greater and fewer people die today from malnutrition than 50 years ago in spite of a doubling of the world's population. New technologies available today—but not yet widely adopted—enable farmers to grow food in hotter, drier, and saltier soils than was previously possible. As new technologies continue to be developed and adopted, it seems almost certain that yields will continue to increase even as the world becomes warmer.

Julian Morris, "The Social Cost of Carbon Underestimates Human Ingenuity, Overestimates Climate Sensitivity," Reason Foundation, August 14, 2015. http://reason.org.

VIEWPOINT

Parker estimates that approximately one-third of the total human population died during the Little Ice Age.

Food Supplies

While the Little Ice Age is proof that cold weather can destroy the world's food supplies, there is no such proof about what will happen if the climate warms significantly, because that has not happened in recent human history. Some people believe that like a very cold climate, a very warm one will also have a negative impact on food production when plants no longer receive the weather they are used to growing in. WHO predicts that increased temperatures and precipitation changes would decrease the production of the staple foods that many of the world's poor

Colder-than-usual weather can have devastating consequences for the world's food supply. In 2012, for example, a cold snap in Greece left orange groves covered with icicles and frozen dew, ruining the entire orange crop for local farmers.

rely on, and this would cause malnutrition. The IPCC also predicts that in most parts of the world, climate change could decrease overall food production.

Others believe that increased temperatures and carbon dioxide will actually be good for crops in many places. Plants grow through photosynthesis, and they use carbon from the air for that growth, so higher carbon dioxide levels theoretically means increased plant growth. Craig D. Idso and Keith E. Idso from the Center for the Study of Carbon Dioxide and Global Change insist:

"With more CO_2 [carbon dioxide] in the air, literally thousands of experiments have *proven*, beyond any doubt, that plants grow bigger and better in almost every conceivable way."[48]

—Craig D. Idso and Keith E. Idso are researchers at the Center for the Study of Carbon Dioxide and Global Change.

It is an indisputable *fact* that carbon dioxide is one of the basic building blocks of life, comprising the major "food" of nearly all plants on earth. With more CO_2 [carbon dioxide] in the air, literally thousands of experiments have *proven*, beyond any doubt, that plants grow bigger and better in almost every conceivable way, and they do it more *efficiently*, with respect to the availability of important natural resources, and more *effectively*, in the face of various environmental constraints. And when plants benefit, so do all of the animals that depend upon them for their sustenance, including us humans.[48]

A number of studies have proved that increased carbon dioxide can benefit plants. One such study was published in 2013 in *Geophysical Research Letters*. The researchers found that there was a 14 percent increase in atmospheric carbon dioxide between 1982 and 2010. They hypothesized that this should have meant an increase in the world's plant growth. To test their hypothesis, they used satellite data on a number of warm, dry parts of the world, including parts of Australia, North America, and Africa. They found that green foliage cover increased by 11 percent during this time, helping to support the theory that increased carbon dioxide did increase plant growth.

An examination of history reveals that climate changes can have a major impact on human society. NASA explains that changes in the climate have always challenged humankind and that people have faced those changes with varying degrees of success. Overall, it says that climate change has been responsible for both the rise and fall of civilizations. The predicted future changes in the world's climate are likely to challenge humankind again. NASA warns, "As our climate changes, we will have to learn to adapt. The faster the climate changes, the harder it could be."[49] There is a great deal of uncertainty about how much adaptation will be required and how human health and well-being will be affected.

Are More Regulations Needed to Help Halt Climate Change?

In 1997 representatives from more than 150 countries—including the United States—met in Kyoto, Japan, with the goal of negotiating an international treaty to reduce greenhouse gas emissions. They acknowledged that greenhouse gases are contributing to climate change and that it is desirable to come to an agreement on how to reduce emissions. After days of discussion, the participating nations agreed to cut their emissions by a specific percentage. Many people were hopeful that this treaty would be a big step in mitigating the threat of climate change.

However, while the meeting at Kyoto demonstrated that there is widespread global concern about emissions and climate change, it also revealed that the topic of regulation to stop climate change is an extremely controversial one. While the representatives at Kyoto were able to agree on a treaty, actually creating and enforcing regulations to address climate change proved to be far more difficult. In order to even become binding, the Kyoto Protocol had to be ratified by at least fifty-five countries, and these countries had to account for a certain percentage of worldwide emissions. Because of continuing disagreement, ratification did not happen until eight years later. A lack of agreement within and between nations also meant that the Kyoto Protocol was revised, edited, and even unratified by major industrial nations, leaving its final form much weaker than its creators had hoped. For example, China, the country with the most emissions, was not part of the treaty, and the United States, another country responsible for a large percentage of greenhouse gases, pulled out in 2001. Many people believe that the Kyoto agreement was largely ineffective. In 2015 representatives from around the world met in Paris for another attempt at an international agreement. However, critics are afraid that like the Kyoto agreement, the Paris one will end up having little effect because there is so much disagreement on the issue of regulation.

Reducing Emissions

One of the most commonly advocated solutions to climate change is to create regulations requiring the reduction of emissions. On an international level, this was the main goal of the Kyoto agreement and also the Paris one. Advocates of this strategy insist that if the world does not reduce its overall emissions, it may experience catastrophic climate change. The IPCC warns, "Continued emission of greenhouse gases will cause further warming and long-lasting changes in all components of the climate system, increasing the likelihood of severe, pervasive and irreversible impacts for people and ecosystems."[50] It says that if the world can substantially reduce its emissions, these severe impacts can be alleviated, and the threat to humankind will be significantly lessened. "Things are going to have to change if we do want to control climate change," says IPCC report author Leon Clarke. "If we do nothing, temperatures will continue to rise."[51] In its most recent report, the IPCC states that in order to reduce the chance of catastrophic climate change, by midcentury the world needs to lower greenhouse gas emissions by 40 percent to 70 percent compared to 2010. In addition, it says the goal should be near-zero emissions by the end of the century.

> "Continued emission of greenhouse gases will cause further warming and long-lasting changes in all components of the climate system."[50]
>
> —The IPCC is the leading international body for the assessment of climate change.

Advocates of emissions reductions believe that the biggest impact will come from reducing emissions from power plants. According to the EPA, in the United States, power generation is the biggest source of greenhouse gas emissions. The EPA reports that in 2013, electricity production caused about 31 percent of all US greenhouse gas emissions. In 2015 president Barack Obama introduced the Clean Power Plan, which aims to significantly reduce carbon emissions by power plants. Obama explains:

> There have never been federal limits on the amount of carbon that power plants can dump into the air. Think about

that. We limit the amount of toxic chemicals like mercury and sulfur and arsenic in our air or our water—and we're better off for it. But existing power plants can still dump unlimited amounts of harmful carbon pollution into the air. For the sake of our kids and the health and safety of all Americans, that has to change. For the sake of the planet, that has to change.[52]

Although the Clean Power Plan has not yet been implemented, its goal is to reduce emissions by 32 percent below 2005 levels by 2030. This will be accomplished in a number of ways, including improving fossil fuel power plants to significantly reduce their carbon pollution and increasing power generation from clean sources such as wind and solar power.

Others contend that reducing emissions will not stop climate change. They argue that there is already so much greenhouse

In 2015 President Barack Obama (pictured) introduced the Clean Power Plan, which aims to reduce power plant carbon emissions by 32 percent below 2005 levels by 2030.

The 2015 Paris Climate Conference Was a Success

In 2015 representatives from 195 nations attended a climate conference in Paris, where they negotiated and signed the Paris Agreement. Signatories agreed to take a number of actions to address climate change, including substantially reducing their greenhouse gas emissions. US president Barack Obama praises the agreement as a victory in the war against climate change.

> In my first inaugural address, I committed this country to the tireless task of combating climate change and protecting this planet for future generations. Two weeks ago, in Paris, I said before the world that we needed a strong global agreement to accomplish this goal—an enduring agreement that reduces global carbon pollution and sets the world on a course to a low-carbon future. A few hours ago, we succeeded. We came together around the strong agreement the world needed. We met the moment. . . . Make no mistake, the Paris agreement establishes the enduring framework the world needs to solve the climate crisis. It creates the mechanism, the architecture, for us to continually tackle this problem in an effective way.

Barack Obama, "Statement by the President on the Paris Climate Agreement," White House, December 12, 2015. www.whitehouse.gov.

gas in the atmosphere that the earth is on an irreversible path to a changing climate. NASA explains why reducing emissions now is unlikely to stop climate change. It says, "Carbon dioxide, the heat-trapping greenhouse gas that has driven recent global warming, lingers in the atmosphere for hundreds of years, and the planet (especially the oceans) takes a while to respond to warming. So even if we stopped emitting all greenhouse gases today, global warming and climate change will continue to affect future generations." While NASA and others do believe that emissions reductions may make climate change less severe, they do not think it is possible to completely stop climate change. NASA insists, "Humanity is 'committed' to some level of climate change."[53]

Another critique of emissions reductions comes from those who believe that climate change has nothing to do with human activities such as power generation. Some people believe that humans are not the cause of climate change, and they argue that it is thus impossible for humans to do anything to stop it. Geologist E. Kirsten Peters insists that climate change on earth is an ongoing and natural cycle and that the current period of warming would be occurring even if humans had never discovered agriculture or industry and started to emit greenhouse gases. As a result, she believes that efforts to stop climate change are futile. She insists,

The 2015 Paris Climate Conference Was a Failure

Following the 2015 Paris climate conference (COP21), a group of scientists wrote a letter to the *Independent* newspaper in which they criticized the agreement reached there. They insist that the agreement has too many flaws to be effective and that celebrating it as a success is giving people false hope.

The hollow cheering of success at the end of COP21 agreement proved yet again that people will hear what they want to hear and disregard the rest. What people wanted to hear was that an agreement had been reached on climate change that would save the world while leaving lifestyles and aspirations unchanged. What they disregarded were the deadly flaws lying just beneath its veneer of success. As early as the third page of the draft agreement is the acknowledgment that its CO_2 target won't keep the global temperate rise below 2 deg C, the level that was once set as the critical safe limit. The solution it proposes is not to agree on an urgent mechanism to ensure immediate cuts in emissions, but to kick the can down the road.

Paul Beckwith et al., letter to the editor, *Independent* (London), January 8, 2016. www.independent.co.uk.

VIEWPOINT

"Regardless of American energy policies and our greenhouse gas emissions, changes in climate . . . are going to be a part of Earth's future, just as they have been the bedrock of the past."[54]

Because of the widespread belief that some level of climate change is inevitable, many people argue that although it is important to try and reduce the effects of climate change through actions such as reducing emissions, society should also put significant resources into regulations that will help it adapt to the coming changes. Some examples of adaptation given by the EPA include breeding food crops that are more tolerant of weather extremes, promoting shoreline protection systems that account for a rising sea, expanding green spaces in order to moderate heat, and improving emergency response plans for storms and other weather extremes.

Regulation and Economic Growth

Other than adaptation, most of the proposed regulations to address climate change involve reducing society's dependence on fossil fuels. However, some critics argue that trying to reduce the use of fossil fuels will be so expensive and restrictive to businesses that it could harm society even more than climate change. They argue that cheap, reliable energy from fossil fuels is essential to economic growth. Further, they insist that this economic growth is what allows people to have a good quality of life. Journalist Eduardo Porter explains that an examination of history reveals that periods of economic growth are associated with improvements in human health and well-being, while periods without this growth are associated with poverty and oppression. He says, "Economic development was indispensable to end slavery. It was a critical precondition for the empowerment of women. Indeed, democracy would not have survived without it." In contrast, he says, "Zero growth gave us Genghis Khan and the Middle Ages, conquest and subjugation. It fostered an order in which the only mechanism to get ahead was to plunder one's neighbor."[55] Porter and others worry that without economic growth, society will collapse. The International Energy Agency agrees that carbon-based energy is an important part of modern life, and it is extremely unrealistic to think about reducing the use of fossil fuels enough to impact climate change. The agency says, "Current short, mid- and long-term projections for global energy demand still point to fossil fuels being combusted in quantities incompatible with levels required to stabilise greenhouse gas (GHG) concentrations at safe levels in the atmosphere."[56]

Clean energy advocates contend that society can reduce its use of fossil fuels without causing the collapse of civilization. At the Paris climate talks in 2015, Obama made a speech in which he stated that over the past seven years, the United States has substantially increased its use of renewable energy as a replacement for fossil fuels; for example, increasing wind power threefold and solar power more than twenty-fold. As

Pictured are solar panels at a US solar power plant. The United States has increased its use of wind power and solar power and thereby lowered its carbon pollution to the lowest level in almost twenty years.

a result of investing in these types of energy, Obama says, US carbon pollution has reached the lowest level in almost twenty years. However, at the same time, he maintains that economic output is at an all-time high. According to Obama, this disproves the argument that moving to renewable energy will be economically harmful. In addition, he insists that this trend is happening around the world. He states, "Last year, the global economy grew while global carbon emissions from burning fossil fuels stayed flat. And what this means can't be overstated. We have broken the old arguments for inaction. We have proved that strong economic growth and a safer environment no longer have to conflict with one another; they can work in concert with one another."[57] Germany is another country that has successfully reduced its use of fossil fuels without stopping economic growth. According to a *New York Times* report, in 2014, 27.8 percent of Germany's power came from renewable sources.

Carbon Capture

Although the use of renewable energy is increasing, doing so is challenging for most countries. As a result, some people believe that since it is such a challenge for society to reduce its use of carbon-based fuels, the best solution is to continue using them but require businesses to eliminate emissions through a process called carbon capture. This involves capturing carbon dioxide from power plants and other places where it is produced and storing it, rather than letting it be released into the atmosphere. Most storage plans involve storing carbon underground. Carbon capture and storage has not yet been proved effective for large-scale use, but many people are hopeful about the potential of this technology. Professor of geosystem science at Oxford University Myles Allen argues that it is clearly the best solution; however, he points out that capture is expensive, so businesses are unlikely to use it unless required to do so. He insists, "Ultimately, the only way we will solve climate change is by making carbon capture mandatory."[58] The EPA discusses how effective carbon capture could be if implemented on a large scale. It says:

CCS [carbon dioxide capture and sequestration] technologies are currently available and can dramatically reduce (by 80–90%) CO_2 emissions from power plants that burn fossil fuels. Applied to a 500 MW [megawatt, a unit of power] coal-fired power plant, which emits roughly 3 million tons of CO_2 per year, the amount of GHG emissions avoided (with a 90% reduction efficiency) would be equivalent to:

- Planting more than 62 million trees, and waiting at least 10 years for them to grow.

- Avoiding annual electricity-related emissions from more than 300,000 homes.[59]

Some advocates of carbon capture think that in the future, the technology may even allow scientists to capture and store some of the carbon dioxide that is already in the atmosphere.

Critics of carbon capture argue that although the theory is good, in reality the technology is prohibitively expensive and plagued with problems. Greenpeace insists that it has simply not been proved successful on the large scale that is necessary to make a difference to carbon emissions. The organization says, "In fact, the world has yet to see a fully integrated CCS project in the power sector come online. What we have seen, however, is a series of high profile projects cancellations and the floundering of industry efforts to mainstream the technology."[60] In addition to difficulties successfully using the technology on a large scale, critics cite safety concerns. They fear that storing large amounts of carbon underground could create so much pressure that it could cause earthquakes, causing the carbon to leak back into the water and atmosphere. Not only would that threaten human health, but it would also make the technology ineffective. In 2012 researchers from Stanford University published a study on carbon storage in which they confirmed that this is likely in most parts of the world, and they conclude that encouraging carbon capture as a solution to climate change does not seem to be a good policy because it is both too expensive and too risky.

Deforestation

Some conservationists point out that there is also a natural way to reduce carbon in the air, which is through the world's forests. They argue that regulations to stop deforestation should be a major priority in the fight against climate change. Limiting deforestation could help reduce climate change in two ways. First, it would greatly reduce global greenhouse gas emissions. While discussions about climate change often focus on fossil fuel emissions, deforestation actually plays a large role too, contributing an estimated 10 percent to 15 percent of the world's total emissions. According to the Nature Conservancy, that is more emissions than from all of the world's planes, trains, and automobiles combined. So reducing deforestation would help significantly reduce overall emissions. Second, it would help address climate change by impacting existing carbon dioxide levels. Senior fellow with the Center for Global Development in Washington, DC, Frances Seymour explains:

"Standing forests soak up carbon into vegetation and soil, providing a safe and natural Carbon Capture and Storage (CCS) technology."[61]

—Frances Seymour is a senior fellow with the Center for Global Development in Washington, DC.

Standing forests soak up carbon into vegetation and soil, providing a safe and natural Carbon Capture and Storage (CCS) technology. If we were to stop tropical deforestation tomorrow, allow damaged forests to grow back, and protect mature forests, the resulting reduction in emissions and removal of carbon from the atmosphere could equal up to one-third of current global emissions from all sources.[61]

Critics contend that while passing regulations to stop deforestation might help slow climate change, it would be a bad policy because it would be economically harmful to many people. Deforestation usually occurs because people need land on which to grow crops or build houses, or because they need the money

Deforestation contributes to increased levels of greenhouse gases, but efforts to stop the practice could pose an economic hardship for many people who need land on which to grow crops. Here, workers harvest rice in Bangladesh on a deforested hilltop.

they can earn by selling wood or other forest resources. For many of the world's poor, these activities are vital to their survival. G. Thomas Farmer, an expert on climate and the environment, explains that survival is much more important to many people than addressing climate change. He says, "It's difficult to convince the residents of the Amazon basin, Indonesia, and other tropical regions of the world to stop cutting down trees when the forests are worth more dead than alive."[62] He points out that cutting down forests helps people earn money by allowing them to sell wood or charcoal or to create farmland, while conservation does the opposite; it costs them money.

From regulations about deforestation to limits on emissions, debate on the topic of climate change is fierce. In a 2015 speech, director-general of WHO Margaret Chan insists that society must

> "A ruined planet cannot sustain human lives in good health. A healthy planet and healthy people are two sides of the same coin."[63]
>
> —Margaret Chan is the director-general of WHO.

address the issue. She points out that the health of humankind is inextricably linked to the planet and warns, "A ruined planet cannot sustain human lives in good health. A healthy planet and healthy people are two sides of the same coin."[63] Like Chan, many people believe that climate change is a serious threat to the health of the planet and humankind, and they insist that society must take action to stop it. However, while most people agree that a healthy planet and healthy people are a desirable goal, many disagree that increased regulations are the best way to maintain that health. What most people do agree on is that the climate directly impacts the life of every person on earth. This means that no matter what society does—or does not do—about climate change, the potential consequences could be life changing.

Introduction: A Changing World

1. Anote Tong, interviewed by Kenneth R. Weiss, "Leader of Island Nation Advocates Exit Strategy for Rising Seas," *National Geographic*, March 10, 2015. http://news.nationalgeo graphic.com.
2. National Aeronautics and Space Administration, "Climate Change: How Do We Know?" http://climate.nasa.gov.
3. European Environment Agency, "Climate Change," February 24, 2016. www.eea.europa.eu.
4. US Environmental Protection Agency, "Climate Change: Basic Information." www3.epa.gov.

Chapter 1: What Are the Facts?

5. National Aeronautics and Space Administration, "Climate Change."
6. National Aeronautics and Space Administration, "The Balance of Power in the Earth-Sun System." www.nasa.gov.
7. John T. Abatzoglou et al., "A Primer on Global Climate-Change Science," in *Climate Change: What It Means for Us, Our Children, and Our Grandchildren*, ed. Joseph F.C. DiMento and Pamela Doughman. Cambridge, MA: MIT Press, 2014, p. 25.
8. National Oceanic and Atmospheric Administration, "Ocean Exploration Facts: Weather and Climate," *Ocean Explorer*, June 21, 2013. http://oceanexplorer.noaa.gov.
9. Quoted in World Meteorological Organization, "Greenhouse Gas Concentrations Hit Yet Another Record," press release, November 9, 2015. www.wmo.int.
10. Intergovernmental Panel on Climate Change, *Climate Change 2014: Synthesis Report. Contribution of Working Groups I, II, and III to the Fifth Assessment Report of the Intergovernmental Panel on Climate Change*, ed. Core Writing Team, R.K. Pachauri, and L.A. Meyer, 2014. http://ar5-syr.ipcc.ch.
11. National Geographic Society, "Encyclopedic Entry: Climate Change." http://education.nationalgeographic.org.
12. Quoted in Joby Warrick and Chris Mooney, "196 Countries Approve Historic Climate Agreement," *Washington Post*, December 12, 2015. www.washingtonpost.com.

Chapter 2: Is Climate Change a Serious Problem?

13. National Aeronautics and Space Administration, "Frequently Asked Questions," *Global Climate Change: Vital Signs of the Planet*. http://climate.nasa.gov.
14. E. Kirsten Peters, *The Whole Story of Climate: What Science Reveals About the Nature of Endless Change*. Amherst, NY: Prometheus, 2012, p. 10.
15. G. Thomas Farmer, *Modern Climate Change Science: An Overview of Today's Climate Change Science*. New York: Springer, 2015, p. 4.
16. Farmer, *Modern Climate Change Science*, p. 13.
17. National Climate Assessment, "Sea Level Rise," 2014. http://nca2014.globalchange.gov.
18. John D. Sutter, "You're Making This Island Disappear," CNN, June 2015. www.cnn.com.
19. Quoted in Rob Taylor, "Pacific Islands Take Steps to Counter Rising Sea Levels," *Wall Street Journal*, December 1, 2015. www.wsj.com.
20. Kennedy Warne, "Will Pacific Island Nations Disappear as Seas Rise? Maybe Not," *National Geographic*, February 13, 2015. http://news.nationalgeographic.com.
21. National Climate Assessment, "Extreme Weather," 2014. http://nca2014.globalchange.gov.
22. Quoted in Peter Miller, "Extreme Weather: Weather Gone Wild," *National Geographic*, September 2012. http://ngm.nationalgeographic.com.
23. Craig D. Idso, Robert M. Carter, and S. Fred Singer, eds., "Climate Change Reconsidered II: Physical Science," Nongovernmental International Panel on Climate Change, 2013. www.nipccreport.org.
24. Bjorn Lomborg, "The Alarming Thing About Climate Alarmism," *Wall Street Journal*, February 1, 2015. www.wsj.com.
25. Idso et al., "Climate Change Reconsidered II."

Chapter 3: Will Climate Change Threaten the Survival of Plants and Animals?

26. Quoted in Emma Marris, "How a Few Species Are Hacking Climate Change," *National Geographic*, May 6, 2014. http://news.nationalgeographic.com.

27. Quoted in Brian Vastag, "Up and Up: Plants and Animals Migrating as Climate Changes," *Washington Post*, August 18, 2011. www.washingtonpost.com.

28. Quoted in Patrick Barkham, "Endangered Butterfly Defies Climate Change with New Diet and Habitat," *Guardian* (Manchester), April 7, 2014. www.theguardian.com.

29. Chris D. Thomas, "The Anthropocene Could Raise Biological Diversity," *Nature*, October 2, 2013. www.nature.com.

30. William deBuys, *A Great Aridness: Climate Change and the Future of the American Southwest*. New York: Oxford University Press, 2011, pp. 289–90.

31. Lee Hannah, *Climate Change Biology*, 2nd ed. London: Elsevier, 2015, p. 101.

32. Intergovernmental Panel on Climate Change, *Climate Change 2014*.

33. Center for Biological Diversity, "The Extinction Crisis." www.biologicaldiversity.org.

34. Hannah, *Climate Change Biology*, p. 74.

35. US Global Change Research Program, "National Climate Assessment: Ecosystems, Biodiversity, and Ecosystem Services," 2014. http://nca2014.globalchange.gov.

36. Ocean Portal Team, reviewed by Jennifer Bennett, Smithsonian National Museum of Natural History, "Ocean Acidification," Smithsonian Ocean Portal. http://ocean.si.edu.

37. Hannah, *Climate Change Biology*, p. 266.

38. Quoted in Louise Gray, "Extinction of Millions of Species 'Greatly Exaggerated,'" *Telegraph* (London), January 24, 2013. www.telegraph.co.uk.

Chapter 4: Will Climate Change Impair Human Health and Well-Being?

39. Quoted in NPR, "Impossible Choice Faces America's First 'Climate Refugees,'" May 19, 2013. www.npr.org.

40. Suzanne Goldenberg, "America's First Climate Refugees," *Guardian* (Manchester), May 13, 2013. www.theguardian.com.

41. Intergovernmental Panel on Climate Change, "Climate Change 2014: Impacts, Adaptation, and Vulnerability, Summary for Policymakers," 2014. www.ipcc.ch.

42. Maria Neira, "Climate Change: An Opportunity for Public Health," World Health Organization, September 14, 2014. www.who.int.

43. Indur M. Goklany, "Unhealthy Exaggeration: The WHO Report on Climate Change," Global Warming Policy Foundation, 2014. www.thegwpf.org.

44. Richard A. Matthew, "Climate Change and Human Security," in *Climate Change: What It Means for Us, Our Children, and Our Grandchildren*, ed. Joseph F.C. DiMento and Pamela Doughman. Cambridge, MA: MIT Press, 2014, p. 268.

45. Quoted in John Schwartz, "Scientists Study Links Between Climate Change and Extreme Weather," *New York Times*, November 5, 2015. www.nytimes.com.

46. Peters, *The Whole Story of Climate*, p. 19.

47. Geoffrey Parker, "Lessons from the Little Ice Age," *New York Times*, March 22, 2014. www.nytimes.com.

48. Craig D. Idso and Keith E. Idso, "Energy, Carbon Dioxide, and Earth's Future: Pursuing the Prudent Path," *CO_2 Science*, 1999. www.co2science.org.

49. National Aeronautics and Space Administration, "Responding to Climate Change." http://climate.nasa.gov.

Chapter 5: Are More Regulations Needed to Help Halt Climate Change?

50. Intergovernmental Panel on Climate Change, *Climate Change 2014*.

51. Quoted in Andrea Thompson, "Major Greenhouse Gas Reductions Needed by 2050: IPCC," Climate Central, April 13, 2014. www.climatecentral.org.

52. Barack Obama, "Remarks by the President in Announcing the Clean Power Plan," White House, August 3, 2015. www.whitehouse.gov.

53. National Aeronautics and Space Administration, "Responding to Climate Change."

54. Peters, *The Whole Story of Climate*, pp. 10–11.

55. Eduardo Porter, "Imagining a World Without Growth," *New York Times*, December 1, 2015. www.nytimes.com.

56. International Energy Agency, "Carbon Capture and Storage." www.iea.org.

57. Barack Obama, "Remarks by President Obama at the First Session of COP21," White House, November 30, 2015. www .whitehouse.gov.
58. Myles Allen, "Carbon Capture Is the Best Answer to Climate Change," *New York Times*, June 1, 2014. www.nytimes .com.
59. US Environmental Protection Agency, "Carbon Dioxide Capture and Sequestration," February 23, 2016. www3.epa.gov.
60. Greenpeace, "Carbon Capture and Storage Won't Save the Climate," November 1, 2015. www.greenpeace.org.
61. Frances Seymour, "In the Fight to Stop Climate Change, Forests Are a Vital Weapon," *Guardian* (Manchester), October 6, 2015. www.theguardian.com.
62. Farmer, *Modern Climate Change Science*, p. 38.
63. Margaret Chan, "WHO Director-General Addresses Event on Climate Change and Health," World Health Organization, December 8, 2015. www.who.int.

Center for Climate and Energy Solutions

2101 Wilson Blvd., Suite 550
Arlington, VA 22201
phone: (703) 516-4146 • fax: (703) 516-9551
e-mail: press@c2es.org
website: www.c2es.org

The Center for Climate and Energy Solutions is a nonprofit organization working to address the challenges of energy and climate change. It is committed to advancing safe, reliable, and affordable energy for the world while protecting the climate.

Center for the Study of Carbon Dioxide and Global Change

PO Box 25697
Tempe, AZ 85285-5697
phone: (480) 966-3719
e-mail: contactus@co2science.org
website: http://co2science.org

The Center for the Study of Carbon Dioxide and Global Change was created to disseminate reports and commentary about new developments related to the consequences of rising carbon dioxide levels. It publishes the magazine CO_2 *Science*, which contains editorials and reviews of scientific journal articles.

Environmental Defense Fund

257 Park Ave. S.
New York, NY 10010
phone: (800) 684-3322
website: www.edf.org

The Environmental Defense Fund's mission is to preserve the natural systems that life depends on. The organization believes society must take action or climate change will have catastrophic effects. The organization's website has information about what it believes are the most effective ways to address the problem.

Intergovernmental Panel on Climate Change (IPCC)

c/o World Meteorological Organization
7bis Avenue de la Paix
C.P. 2300
CH-1211 Geneva 2, Switzerland
phone: +41-22-730-8208/54/84 • fax: +41-22-730-8025/13
e-mail: IPCC-Sec@wmo.int
website: www.ipcc.ch

The IPCC is the leading international body for the assessment of climate change. Thousands of scientists from all over the world contribute to the work of the IPCC on a voluntary basis. Its website includes reports, graphics, and speeches about climate change.

National Oceanic and Atmospheric Association (NOAA)

1401 Constitution Ave. NW, Room 5128
Washington, DC 20230
phone: (301) 713-1208
website: www.noaa.gov

The NOAA researches the conditions of the oceans and the atmosphere and supplies information about atmospheric and weather conditions to the public. Its climate change website contains numerous fact sheets and articles about climate change.

Nongovernmental International Panel on Climate Change (NIPCC)

website: http://climatechangereconsidered.org

The NIPCC is an international panel of scientists and scholars that are not affiliated with any government. It was founded in 2003 due to the belief that the IPCC is too heavily influenced by political interests. Its website contains numerous reports about climate change.

US Environmental Protection Agency (EPA)

1200 Pennsylvania Ave. NW
Washington, DC 20460
phone: (202) 272-0167
website: www.epa.gov

The EPA is the federal agency that works to protect human health and the environment. It performs research, develops environmental regulations, and educates the public about environmental issues. Its website contains numerous articles and fact sheets about climate change.

World Health Organization (WHO)

Avenue Appia 20
1211 Geneva 27
Switzerland
phone: 41 22 791 21 11
website: www.who.int

WHO is an agency of the United Nations that works to monitor and improve health around the world. Its website contains fact sheets and statistics about climate change and human health.

Books

Joseph F.C. DiMento and Pamela Doughman, eds., *Climate Change: What It Means for Us, Our Children, and Our Grandchildren*. Cambridge, MA: MIT Press, 2014.

G. Thomas Farmer, *Modern Climate Change Science: An Overview of Today's Climate Change Science*. New York: Springer, 2015.

Lee Hannah, *Climate Change Biology*, 2nd ed. London: Elsevier, 2015.

E. Kirsten Peters, *The Whole Story of Climate: What Science Reveals About the Nature of Endless Change*. Amherst, NY: Prometheus, 2012.

Internet Sources

Greenpeace, "Carbon Capture and Storage Won't Save the Climate," November 1, 2015. www.greenpeace.org/international/en /campaigns/climate-change/coal/carbon-capture-and-storage.

Nongovernmental International Panel on Climate Change, "Climate Change Reconsidered II: Physical Science: Summary for Policymakers," 2013. www.nipccreport.org/reports/ccr2a/ccr2 physicalscience.html.

US Environmental Protection Agency, "Carbon Dioxide Capture and Sequestration," February 23, 2016. www3.epa.gov/climate change/ccs.

US Global Change Research Program, "National Climate Assessment: Ecosystems, Biodiversity, and Ecosystem Services," 2014. http://nca2014.globalchange.gov.

Websites

Climate Central (www.climatecentral.org). This website contains reports and analyses of climate change research. Topics include weather changes, water security, and sea level rise.

Global Climate Change: Vital Signs of the Planet (http://climate.nasa.gov). Global Climate Change was created by climate experts from NASA and the California Institute of Technology. The website has a blog, articles, facts, and interactive graphics about climate change.

National Climate Assessment (http://nca2014.globalchange.gov). The National Climate Assessment was created by more than three hundred experts and a US federal advisory committee. It contains information about how climate change is impacting the United States and how it is likely to impact the country in the future.

Skeptical Science (www.skepticalscience.com). *Skeptical Science* is a blog that challenges the arguments made by those who deny that climate change is real. It contains numerous articles investigating whether there is any scientific basis behind climate change skepticism.

malaria, 42, 43
Mars, 9
Marshall Islands, 24
Matthew, Richard A., 46
medicines, 35–36
methane, 9, 10
microcephaly, 43–44, **44**
migrations, 31
Miller, Peter, 27
monsoon rains, 5
Morris, Julian, 49
Mount Pinatubo (Philippines), effects of
    eruption, 17

National Aeronautics and Space Administration
    (NASA)
    adaptation by humans to climate change,
        52
    amount of energy produced by sun, 8–9
    effects of reducing greenhouse gases,
        19–20, 56
    on evidence for climate change, 6
    on past climate changes, 8
National Climate Assessment, 22–23, 26, 35,
    46
National Geographic (magazine), 17, 24,
    26–27
National Geographic Society, 14–15
National Institute of Environmental Health
    Sciences, 43
National Oceanic and Atmospheric
    Administration (NOAA)
    Arctic ice in summer, 16
    coral reefs, 38
    increase in intense hurricanes, 27
    role of ocean currents in climate, 10–11
National Snow & Ice Data Center, 16
National Weather Service, 45–46
Nature Climate Change (journal), 22
Nature Conservancy, 62
Neira, Maria, 42
Newtok, Alaska, 41
New York Times (newspaper), 60
nitrous oxide, 9, 10
Nongovernmental International Panel on
    Climate Change (NIPCC), 27–29

Obama, Barack, **55**
    Clean Power Plan, 54–55
    on climate refugees, 24
    on Paris Agreement, 56
    replacements for fossil fuels, 59–60
oceans
    adaptation in Pacific, 24–25

geoengineering, 15
    increase in acidity, 36–38
    increase in temperature, 14
        coral reefs and, 38, **39**
        as response to land surface
            temperatures, 23
        sea turtles and, 34
    as percentage of Earth's surface, 10
    rise in levels
        due to melting ice sheets, 17, 23
        effects of, 4, 22, 23–25
        opinions about, 17, 28
        predicting speed and amount, 21–23
    role of currents in climate, 10–11

Pacific Ocean, 4, 23–25
Paisley, Brad, 27
Paris Agreement (2015)
    disagreement about regulations, 53
    goals, 18, 54
    was failure, 57
    was success, 56
Parker, Geoffrey, 48–50
Parmesan, Camille, 31
Peters, E. Kirsten, 20, 47, 57–58
plants
    ability to adapt, 30–32, 58
    carbon dioxide emissions increase growth,
        51–52
    deforestation, 11, 62–63
    effectiveness of carbon capture compared
        to planting trees, 61
    number of existing species, 39–40
    species extinction, 34–36
    speed of climate change and, 33
polar bears, 30, **32**
Porter, Eduardo, 58–59

quino checkerspot butterflies, 31

rainfall
    flooding due to, 26–27
    forests' role in, 11
    increase in food-borne and waterborne
        diseases, 45
Ripley, S. Dillon, 37
Russia, 46

Sahara Desert, 8, **10**
Science (journal), 31, 36
seas. *See* oceans
Sea Turtle Conservancy, 34
sea turtles, 34
Seymour, Frances, 62

PICTURE CREDITS

ABOUT THE AUTHOR

Andrea C. Nakaya, a native of New Zealand, holds a BA in English and an MA in communications from San Diego State University. She has written and edited more than forty books on current issues. She currently lives in Encinitas, California, with her husband and their two children, Natalie and Shane.